The Way of Love

*A booklet on the real meaning of love,
the essence of true spirituality*

His Divine Grace
Śrīla Bhaktivedānta Nārāyaṇa Mahārāja

OTHER BOOKS BY ŚRĪLA NĀRĀYAṆA MAHĀRĀJA

For further information and free download of all titles, please visit:

www.purebhakti.com

To receive by e-mail, the lectures given by Śrī Śrīmad Bhaktivedānta Nārāyaṇa Mahārāja on his world tours, please subscribe at:

www.harikatha.com

ISBN #81-86737-92-8
Copyright © Gauḍīya Vedānta Publications 2004

Photo of Sri Srimad A.C. Bhaktivedanta Swami Prabhupada, and Syamarani dasi's paintings on p.5 © Bhaktivedanta Book Trust International, Inc. Used with permission

Syamarani dasi's paintings on p.6 and 17 © Syamarani dasi. Used with permission

First printing 25,000
Second printing 50,000
Third printing 50,000
Fourth printing 40,000
Printed at Spectrum Offset Printers, New Delhi, India

Dedication

I beg the mercy of my Gurudeva, *nitya-līlā pravviṣṭa oṁ viṣṇupāda* Śrī Śrīmad Bhakti Prajñāna Keśava Gosvāmī Mahārāja. I offer thousands of humble obeisances unto his lotus feet, and the same humble obeisances unto the lotus feet of my *siksa-guru, nitya-līlā pravviṣṭa oṁ viṣṇupāda* Śrī Śrīmad Bhaktivedānta Svāmī Mahārāja.

In the present day, it was my *siksa-guru* who unlocked the treasure of Vedic wisdom for the entire world. The key to the treasure is in his hands and in my Gurudeva's hands. They have given me their key, and they have ordered me to share that treasure with you all.

Many participated in completing the publication of this booklet in the role of editors, editorial advisors, designers, artists, typists, transcribers, proofreaders and technical assistants. They include: Śrīpāda Bhaktivedānta Mādhava Mahārāja, Śrīpāda Bhaktivedānta Vaikhanas Mahārāja, Atula-kṛṣṇa dāsa, Ānītā dāsī, Bhūdhara dāsa, Brajanātha dāsa, Dhanañjaya dāsa, Giridhārī dāsa, Gaurāṅgi dāsī, Gurūttama dāsa, Jaya-gopāla dāsa, Mahaprābhu dāsa, Nanda-kiśora dāsa, Nandimukhi dāsī, Nāndinī dāsī, Premavatī dāsī, Rādhā-kānta dāsa, Śānti dāsī, Sudarśana dāsa, Sundara-gopāla dāsa, Śyāmarāṇī dāsī, Vaijayantī-mālā dāsī, Vasanti dāsī and Viśvambhara dāsa.

Special thanks to all the book distributors, for helping to bring this publication to our respected readers.

His Divine Grace Śrīla Bhaktivedānta Nārāyaṇa Mahārāja

His Divine Grace Śrīla A.C. Bhaktivedānta Svāmī Prabhupāda

Contents

Preface

The purpose of this booklet is to present the words of those who have realized the sacred truths revealed in ancient Indian scriptures called the Vedas. The word Veda literally means "the final conclusion on all topics related to the transcendental world and all topics related to this world, both ordinary and extraordinary."

The Vedas were compiled thousands of years ago by self-realized saints whose hearts were melting with affection for the suffering souls in this world. Such saints are blessed with pure understanding of the Supreme Truth and the ultimate purpose of life. An example in modern times is the author of *The Way of Love*, the revered Śrīla Bhaktivedānta Nārāyaṇa Mahārāja, whose life is unconditionally dedicated to the ultimate happiness of others.

In this Preface, we would like to share with you the words of another great saint, Śrīla Bhaktivedānta Svāmī Prabhupāda, who is intimately related with the author as an instructing guru and a dear friend. Śrīla Nārāyaṇa Mahārāja, regards Śrīla Prabhupāda as a main inspiration for his regularly traveling the surface of the globe and teaching the way of love. Śrīla Prabhupāda writes:

"The basic principle of the living condition is that we have a general propensity to love someone. No one can live without loving someone else. This propensity is present in every living being. Even an animal like a tiger has this loving propensity at least in a dormant stage, and it is certainly present in the human beings. The missing point, however, is where to repose our love so that everyone can become happy. At the present moment the human society teaches one to love his country or family or his personal self, but there is no information about where to repose the loving propensity so that everyone can become happy.

"In the primary stage a child loves his parents, then his brothers and sisters, and as he daily grows up he begins to love his family, society, community, country, nation or even the whole human society. But the loving propensity is not satisfied even by loving all human society. That loving propensity remains imperfectly fulfilled until we know who is the supreme beloved. Our loving propensity expands just as a vibration of light or air expands, but we do not know where it ends."

Śrīla Prabhupāda continues to explain the problem we face – not knowing how to love. He explains the science of loving every living being perfectly by the process of loving the Supreme Being, known in the Vedas as Kṛṣṇa.

"We have failed to create peace and harmony in human society, even by such great attempts as the United Nations, because we do not know the right method. The method is very simple.

"If we learn how to love Kṛṣṇa, then it is very easy to immediately and simultaneously love every living being. It is like pouring water on the root of a tree or supplying food to one's stomach. The method of pouring water on the root of a tree or supplying foodstuffs to the stomach is universally scientific and practical, as every one of us has experienced. Everyone knows well that when we eat something, or in other words, when we put foodstuffs in the stomach, the energy created by such action is immediately distributed throughout the whole body. Similarly, when we pour water on the root, the energy thus created is immediately distributed throughout the entirety of even the largest tree. It is not possible to water the tree part by part, nor is it possible to feed the different parts of the body separately."

"The root cause of our dissatisfaction is that our dormant loving propensity has not been fulfilled despite our great advancement in the materialistic way of life. We are watering all parts of the tree, but missing the tree's root. We are trying to keep our body fit by all means, but we are neglecting to supply foodstuffs to the stomach.

"Missing the Supreme Self means missing one's self also. Self-realization and realization of the Supreme Soul, known as Lord Śrī Kṛṣṇa, the all-attractive reservoir of love, go together simultaneously. For example, seeing oneself in the morning means seeing the sunrise also; without seeing the sunshine no one can see himself. Relations of the soul, established in relation with the Supreme Soul, are factual relations. The bodily relation is the cause of material bondage, but the relation of the soul is the cause of freedom. This relation of the soul to the soul can be established by the via medium of the relation with the Supersoul. Seeing in the darkness is not seeing. But seeing by the light of the sun means to see the sun and everything else that was unseen in the darkness."

As is true with all Vedic literature, this booklet is meant to teach us how to "turn the one switch that will immediately brighten everything, everywhere." All the histories told herein actually took place. Śrīla Nārāyaṇa Mahārāja has taken them from the parts of the Vedas known as the Purāṇas and Upaniṣads.

The names of all the personalities herein are in the ancient Sanskrit language. Following the tradition of our spiritual preceptors we use standard diacritical markings to indicate the pronunciation of Sanskrit words. Pronounce *ā* like a in father, *ī* like ea in neat, *ū* like oo in root, *ṛ* like ri in.rip, *ṁ* and *ṅ* like ng in hung, *ś* and *ṣ* like sh in shy, and *c* like ch in chap.

Śyāmarāṇī dāsī
Editor

The appearance day of Lord Caitanya
March 6, 2004

The Way of Love

Misplaced Love

There was once a very qualified and beautiful young king named Bhartrihari, who was expert in all the arts. King Bhartrihari married at the age of twenty-five years, and he adored his beautiful newly-wedded wife. Eager to please her, he presented her with a jeweled necklace, the value of which would be over a million dollars by today's standards. He placed the necklace around her neck with his own hands, embraced her and said, "Most dearly beloved, this necklace is very precious. Please always keep it with you."

King Bhartrihari was greatly attracted to his wife, but she had no such attraction to him. Rather, she was attracted to her husband's commander-in-chief, who was also extremely handsome. Therefore, a few days after receiving the excellent necklace, she gave it to the commander-in-chief, desiring to please him.

Although the queen was very attached to the commander-in-chief, he did not feel the same way about her. He was attached to a prostitute. A few days after receiving the necklace, he presented it to that prostitute, desiring to please her. The prostitute did not feel the same way about the commander-in-chief, however, for she was attached to the king. One day she presented that very necklace to the king, desiring to please him. Seeing the necklace, the king became distressed and asked her from where she had gotten it. Frightened, she did not reply. The incensed king said, "If you don't tell me the truth I will cut off your head." The prostitute then revealed the truth of the matter to the king, who left her and took the necklace to the commander-in-chief.

King Bhartrihari asked his commander-in-chief, "Where did you get this? If you tell me the truth I will not harm you, but if you try to conceal it from me I will have your head." The commander-in-chief revealed the truth to him, and at that moment the king realized that there is no true love in this world. He at once made up his mind to give up all his worldly attachments. He left his palace, his kingdom and his opulent attire, and he became a very famous renunciant and spiritualist.

[King Bhartrihari's grief and anger arose from his affection that had turned sour. This was caused by his not knowing that in order to love, one must first embrace the Supreme Love. The misery he tasted due to misunderstanding that Supreme Love, God, is common in this world. Some of us think that He does not exist, some think He is formless and without qualities, and some think there are different Divinities or Gods for those of different faiths. The following reveals how anyone can become free from all suffering caused by animosity, envy and quarrelling by knowing that single one Divine Reality. – ed]

There is Only One Family

All of us are in the family of one God. It is not that there is one God in England, another in America, and still another in India. The Christians, Muslims and Hindus are not worshiping different Gods. The names Allah, Brahma, Jehovah, Kṛṣṇa and Yahweh refer to the same God, called by different names according to differences in language and culture.

If we love the same one God, why do we quarrel? We quarrel because we don't know what real love is. If we have true love and affection for the one Supreme Lord, we will naturally love each other. There is a saying, "God is love and love is God." And in Indian Vedic culture there is a saying, "All should be happy."

Jesus also taught this philosophy. He went to India when he was about sixteen years old, and he visited many places of pilgrimage, like Vṛndāvana, Ayodhyā, South India and Jagannātha Purī. In Purī he saw the deities of Jagannātha, Baladeva and Subhadrā, and he heard Lord Jagannātha (meaning "Lord of the Universe") addressed as Kṛṣṇa. In this part of India, the name Kṛṣṇa is pronounced Kroosna. Because of different languages, Greek and Hebrew, this name became Kroosta, then Krista, and now it is pronounced Christ. Kṛṣṇa, Kroosna, Krista and now Christ – they are the same.

In this universe there is only one God, and He is not Russian, English, German or Spanish. He knows all languages without difficulty, but there is actually no need of knowing them. There is only one real language in the entire world, and that language is called love. Eyes can speak that language, ears and hands can speak and understand it, and a glowing face can tell everything.

God is one, and He is the embodiment of Love. Kṛṣṇa is the original name of God, given in the ancient Vedas, and it means "the all-attractive reservoir of pleasure." All other names, like Supersoul, Buddha, Allah and God, are included within Him.

Unity in Diversity

Although we are all parts and parcels of the same Supreme Lord, we have divided up this Earth, declaring, "This is my country! This is your country!"

Even though we are all individuals, we all depend upon the same sun and we all breathe the same air. This is the principle of unity in diversity. Unity refers to the fact that we are all parts and parcels of the same Supreme Lord Kṛṣṇa, the father of all; and diversity refers to our eternal individual natures. Because this is the eternal reality, we will only find peace and happiness in this reality. Unity in diversity will have no meaning if people have no faith in the Supreme God, or love for Him and all living entities.

Love All Creatures

It is often thought that humans are the only members of God's family, but this is not true. He creates all creatures. They are all His children, so why should we not love them all? The saying "All should be happy" does not only apply to humans.

The Supreme Lord has created cows, and those cows freely and indiscriminately give milk to all. In the Vedas the cow is referred to as *go mātā*, Mother Cow, because she nourishes us with her own milk. It is not stated anywhere in the Bible that we may kill the cow, or any animal. In the original Aramaic language of the Bible, the word "brosimus" has been used more than

Lord Kṛṣṇa plays a melody on His flute, captivating all worlds and creatures. All living entities become stunned in ecstasy.

Kṛṣṇa, the self-effulgent embodiment of love and eternal bliss.

twenty times. "Brosimus" means "food" and it has been translated as "meat". In Old English "meat" did not mean "flesh"; it meant "food". But the English language has changed, and today most people wrongly believe that the Holy Bible supports the eating of animal flesh.

The Old Testament clearly states, "Thou shall not kill." This means we should neither kill humans nor animals. The Koran also does not sanction the slaughtering and eating of cows. The Supreme Lord has not created animals for us to eat. For this purpose He has created fruits, roots, milk, butter, grains and vegetables. He will not be happy if we harm any of His children, what to speak of killing our own mother.

Trees, creepers, hogs and insects are also children of the one Supreme Lord. In Indian Vedic culture it is said that one should not walk on a field after it has been plowed and the seeds have been sown there, for those seeds may die. We should not give pain or suffering to any living being.

We are all children of the Supreme Lord, who is the personification of supreme happiness and the reservoir of supreme happiness for all others. We are part and parcel of that Happiness. The only difference between the Supreme Lord and ourselves is that He is unlimited and we are minute. We are qualitatively one with Him, but unfortunately we have forgotten who we are. We should try to realize this truth. We must not quarrel with those of other religious faiths. The one true religion of all souls is love, and that religion is one without a second. We should love God and also each other, and in this way people can live happily in this world.

Love has a Form

The Vedas explain that the Supreme has a transcendental form and personal qualities, and He performs extraordinary pastimes. He is all-attractive and the possessor of all potency. He is indivisible and one without a second. Although He is one, and although He is everything, He is a person. God: G – generator, the generator of this world; O – operator, the operator of this world, and D – destroyer, the destroyer of this world. He nourishes and supports the entire universe. Vedic sages like Śrīla Vyāsadeva, Nārada Muni and Lord Brahmā have told us that He has a very beautiful form and many millions of transcendental qualities.

If a father has a form, his son will also have a form. If the father has no form or qualities, the son will neither have form nor qualities, nor can he even exist.

It may appear that God is sometimes described as formless in certain scriptures, but when such scriptures use the word "formless", they mean that He has no material form, no material qualities and no material features. His shape and features are spiritual. He is all-powerful, and therefore He has the power to have a form. If He were without form, qualities, power and mercy, He would be nothing. He would be unable to help us or hear our prayers, what to speak of giving us eternal bliss. We don't believe in a God devoid of mercy, power and qualities. If He were without transcendental qualities such as mercy, what value and purpose would there be in worshiping Him?

Both the Bible and the Koran state that He has a form. The Bible states, "God created man in His own image." If He has no image, or form, why does the Bible say this? His image is transcendental; it is not mortal. He has a spiritual body from which He created man. It is also said that Jesus Christ is the Son of God. If the son has form, then his father must also have form.   In fact, He has the most beautiful form. He has all good qualities and He is complete with all potencies.

The Koran states: "Inallah kalaka mein suratihi – Allah, or Kudda, has form, and from that form He has fashioned man." The word "suratihi" means "form" and the name Allah means "the greatest". All universes and all creation are contained within Him, and there is nothing equal to Allah in greatness. The Vedic conception of God confirms this understanding and also says that the Supreme Being, Lord Kṛṣṇa, is both the greatest of the great and the smallest of the small.

The words "formless", "without qualities" and "without features", used in scriptures to describe God, have come from the root words "form", "qualities" and "features". Without the concept of something having form, there can be no concept of something being devoid of form. It must therefore be concluded that the Supreme Original Entity has form, qualities and features; and one of those qualities must be mercy. He is so merciful that He created this entire world – to fulfill our foolish desire to enjoy separately from Him.

Without that Love

Once, a man in a forest heard the sound of a tiger. As he ran in fear, his eyes darted here and there looking for shelter. Finally he came across a "blind well", a well that is no longer in use. Grass and plants had grown over that well and a tree grew beside it. Taking help from two branches of the tree, the man lowered himself into the well, comforted by the thought that he was beyond the tiger's reach. As he descended the well, however, he saw beneath him many snakes. The snakes raised their hoods and hissed, ready to bite him.

As he hung from the two branches he realized that his predicament had only increased. At the bottom of the well there were many poisonous snakes waiting to bite him and at the top a ferocious tiger waited to eat him. He was suffering great anxiety.

Then, two rats – one black and one white – began gnawing the branches onto which he held. It was only a question of time before the branches would be eaten through and he would fall into the pit of snakes. To escape this predicament, he had to either climb out and be eaten by the tiger or descend into the well and be bitten by the snakes. Whatever he chose to do, his fate would be gruesome.

In this very dangerous situation, the man suddenly noticed a honeycomb on the branch of the tree. Because the tree was shaking, some honey was dripping and it just happened to be dripping very close to his face. Taking this opportunity to enjoy, he stuck out his tongue and took that honey into his mouth. He began to relish the flavor, thinking, "Oh, how sweet! How sweet!" Feeling some happiness, he completely forgot the danger he was in.

All the components of this analogy represent our own condition. The man in this story exemplifies all souls who are attached to this world. We are in a dangerous situation, as we may die at any moment, and there is no way for us to be saved by our material endeavors. The snakes represent our many problems, coming at us one after another like waves in an ocean. We think, "Oh, this is the last of my problems. I will be happy as soon as this problem is solved." But sometimes the next wave is larger still, and sometimes many waves, or problems, come at once – five or six at a time. At the top of the well stands the tiger, who represents death, which is waiting for every one of us in this world.

The two branches represent the reactions to our fruitive activities – good and bad, pious and impious. We live our lives experiencing the reactions of our pious and impious activities. Combined together, these reactions comprise the duration of our life, and that duration is being taken away moment by moment. The black rat represents nighttime and the white rat daytime. We are very happy when another day comes and goes, but actually the coming and going of days only means that the duration of our life is being gnawed away.

Amidst so many problems and dangers one drop of honey falls on our tongues, and this drop is likened to the momentary happiness we may feel with friends and relatives of this world.

The Search for Happiness

All living creatures are making a great endeavor, struggling, to attain real everlasting happiness. However, as the Vedas explain, worldly things cannot give us happiness. Regardless of the position a person may hold, he or she remains unfulfilled. Even if one is wealthy, young, beautiful, educated, famous and influential, he still looks for something more to make him happy.

Even the presidents and prime ministers of great nations remain unsatisfied. Throughout history it has been revealed that rich and powerful persons, like Napoleon and the kings and queens of England, France and Germany, were deeply unhappy despite their seemingly advantageous positions. In modern times, we can see this in the lives of Princess Diana and Bill Clinton, to name a few. The little happiness we receive in this world is momentary and mixed with suffering. It is not continuous and eternal, nor is it complete and pure. From the lowest material planet to the highest, there are so many types of misery and no real eternal happiness.

No soul identifying with a material body can be happy. This human life is meant for finding a way out of the prison of this body, which is destined to grow old and die. We want to be happy by satisfying our material bodies, but old age very quickly overtakes us and we lament. The material happiness we receive is not really happiness; it is condensed misery. We do not understand that the soul, which is different from the body and mind, is spiritual, eternal, and full of knowledge and bliss. We can therefore only be truly satisfied by that which is also spiritual, eternal, and full of knowledge and bliss – the Supreme Personality of Godhead and our loving relationship with Him.

Nowadays we are making many inventions and discoveries in areas such as medicine, transportation and communication. We can easily travel from one side of the world to the other in just a few hours. By sitting in our living room we can see what is happening on the other side of the world. We can watch cricket being played in Australia or India and we can see the President of America speaking in the White House in Washington. And, if a person's eyes are defective, surgeons can repair them with parts of eyes taken from a dead body.

However, despite these and other advances, people are suffering more than ever before. We are still not able to prevent old age and death; and we cannot prevent war and terrorism, or the spread of disease. New diseases continue to appear. The advances in science and technology have not brought us happiness. Rather, we have become more fearful, materialistic and greedy.

Why is modern science failing us? The reason is that it is not, in fact, very developed. Scientists cannot see the soul, which has a transcendental form; and they cannot even see the mind, which is material. We think that we are very advanced due to developments in technology, but all we have done is increase the needs of the material body and neglect the needs of the soul. We do not care to love the Supreme Lord, and thus we do not have any real love and affection for each other.

We trust our dogs and cats more than we trust our families and friends. Husbands and wives do not remain together and divorce is common. Parents reject their children and children reject their parents. Almost everyone is interested only in gratifying his own body and mind.

Persons who want to control the endless chain of birth, disease, old age and death can learn to do so from the ancient Vedic culture. Studying modern scientific knowledge will not help. When scientific knowledge develops to a more sophisticated level, people may finally be able to control old age and death. But to attain this level, modern society must learn from our Vedic culture.

A Perfect Question

The Vedas tell an ancient history. There was once a self-realized soul named Yājñavalkya, and he served in the council of the great and celebrated King Janaka. He was very learned in the Vedas and he was fully aware of the presence of the soul and Supersoul within the body.

Yājñavalkya had two wives, Maitreyi and Kātyāyanī. Once, in his old age, he called his two wives and said to them: "We have lived as householders for many years. I have amassed vast amounts of gold and many cows, and I have also given each of you several children. I now want to divide all my property between you so that you will be happy for the rest of your lives. After I have done this, please permit me to go to the forest to meditate deeply on the Supreme Personality of Godhead."

Hearing this, Kātyāyanī became happy and said: "Your goal, which is very wonderful, is to meditate on the Supreme Lord. You are my husband, and I shall assist you in doing this."

Maitreyi gave a different response. She said, "I have a question, and after you have answered it you can go with a glad heart. You are going to the forest because you are not satisfied with all the gold and property you have accumulated during your life, or with your wives, children and friends. So do you think these things will then make us happy?"

Yājñavalkya replied: "You are truly my devoted wife. By asking this question you have greatly pleased me. The answer to this question is discussed in all the Vedas. Gold and property cannot give real happiness. Position in society, learning, reputation, friendship and family can never make one truly happy. Money and whatever it may buy in this world cannot give us what we hanker for. We are parts and parcels of the Supreme Lord and He is the reservoir of all happiness. Therefore we can find happiness only in Him. To serve Him is actual happiness, whereas the happiness we taste in this world is minute and also perishable. Lord Kṛṣṇa is an ocean of transcendental tasteful relationships and the embodiment of supreme happiness. He alone can satisfy us; so I wish to go now to the forest to attain Him."

The Path to Happiness

If we want to be truly happy, we must engage in the practice of serving God. In the Vedas this process is called *bhakti-yoga*, or connecting with the Supreme Lord by serving Him. By considering His happiness first, a person automatically becomes happy and peaceful. He does not harm other creatures, be they animals or humans, and as a result he can live peacefully with all.

Devotion to God has three stages of development: the stage of practice, the stage of awakening spiritual ecstasy, and the stage of fully blossomed ecstasy called pure love.

To achieve pure love, we begin at the stage of practice. In this age of quarrel and hypocrisy, called Kali-yuga, the most powerful spiritual practice and the best method to find happiness is to chant the name of the Supreme Lord. His name is non-different from Him and it contains all of His potencies as well as His sweet forms and pastimes. This will be realized fully at the stage of pure love. Chanting the holy name of God cleanses the heart of all unhealthy desires and tendencies, leaving one feeling tranquil and connected to Him.

The Vedic text named *Kali-santarana Upaniṣad* states: "In this age of quarrel and hypocrisy the only means of deliverance is chanting the holy name of the Lord. There is no other way. There is no other way. There is no other way." The names of the Lord can be chanted as follows:

Hare Kṛṣṇa Hare Kṛṣṇa
Kṛṣṇa Kṛṣṇa Hare Hare
Hare Rāma Hare Rāma
Rāma Rāma Hare Hare

Mantra of Divine Love

Water, air and practically everything is polluted these days. As the oceans are polluted by poisons, thus poisoning both the fish and the fish eaters, material sound vibration also pollutes and poisons the atmosphere. People spray poisons to kill insects, thus poisoning the grains and those who eat them. Similarly, material sound vibration in the form of abuses, criticism of others, quarrelling and so forth, and in fact any material vibration, pollutes the minds, senses and hearts of everyone throughout the world. We can counteract this pollution and pain by chanting the Hare Kṛṣṇa *mantra*.

An example may be given of a big pond. If you take a stone and throw it into a pond, the waves that are created will touch all edges of the pond. This universe is like that pond. Chanting Hare Kṛṣṇa Hare Kṛṣṇa Kṛṣṇa Kṛṣṇa Hare Hare, Hare Rāma Hare Rāma Rāma Rāma Hare Hare creates many waves of spiritual vibration. Those waves touch everything – up to the end of the world – moving here and there and purifying the entire universe from all pollution.

Lord Kṛṣṇa is inconceivably powerful. He can create the entire universe in a second and then destroy it, and again He can create many worlds. He has invested all His mercy, power

Śrī Caitanya Mahāprabhu and His associate Lord Nityānanda brought the chanting of Hare Kṛṣṇa to this world. They are likened to the sun and the moon, and they have arisen simultaneously to dissipate the darkness of ignorance and thus wonderfully bestow benedictions upon all.

and opulence in His names, and thus they are also unlimitedly powerful. They very quickly travel throughout the universe as spiritual sound vibrations, and the pollution gradually disappears.

Trees, creepers, animals and insects cannot speak. They cannot understand our language. Still, everyone – not only humans, but all creatures throughout this universe – will be touched by the powerful holy name, whether they are aware of it or not. If one touches fire knowingly or unknowingly, he will feel its effects. Similarly, these holy names will inspire and purify all living beings, whether they are aware or not. Trees, grasses and humans all become fortunate when they hear about Kṛṣṇa, and even the creatures in the jungles are gradually liberated from suffering.

If we chant loudly, all our senses will be purified, and there will be nothing to criticize and no unhappy memories. By material endeavors we cannot control the unhappy and unbeneficial thoughts that enter our minds, but they are conquered very easily by chanting. Gradually our hearts will be cleansed by such chanting, and then we will realize that our real self-interest – the Soul of our souls – is Lord Kṛṣṇa. Therefore, if we serve Him, we and the entire world are benefited.

"God is Love and Love is God"
Chant the Hare Kṛṣṇa Mantra and be Happy

For further information, please visit:

www.purebhakti.com
for news, updates and free downloads of books and lectures.

www.harikatha.com
to receive by e-mail, the lectures given by
Śrī Śrīmad Bhaktivedānta Nārāyaṇa Mahārāja
on his world tours.

www.pbwebcast.com
to watch and hear classes online,
or get links and schedule updates for live webcasts.

Global Contacts

For more information, please contact us at the listings below:
For updates, please visit our website: **www.purebhakti.com (www.purebhakti.com/centers)**

AMERICA: • **California** - **Badger:** Nanda Gopal dāsa <u>Tel</u>: (001) 559-337 2448 <u>Email</u>: nandagopal@purebhakti.com - **Bay Area San Francisco:** Hrdayagovinda dāsa E-mail: <u>hrdayagovinda@yahoo.com</u> Telephone: (510) 478-4063 • **Florida - Alachua:** Iśa dāsa <u>Tel</u>: (001) 386-462 9029 <u>Email</u>: isadasa@hotmail.com - **Miami:** Institute of Vaiṣṇavism, 934 N. University Drive #102 <u>Tel</u>: (001) 754-245 2345 **Orlando:** Latika dāsī <u>Tel</u>: (001) 407-366 8582 <u>Email</u>: latika108@yahoo.com • **Hawaii - Hilo:** Gopa-vrndapāla dāsa <u>Tel</u>: (001) 808-935 7247 **Maui:** Chiranjiva dāsa and Shamapriya dāsī, 1140 Freitas place, Makawao, Maui Hi 96768 <u>Tel</u>: (001) 808-573 6968 <u>Email</u>: shamapriya108@yahoo.com • **Texas - Houston:** IGVS, Kṛṣṇa dāsa, 16119 Abergreen Trail, Houston, TX 77095 <u>Tel</u>: (001) 281-550 2940 <u>Email</u>: kris4basics@hotmail.com • **New Jersey:** Vinay Krishna dāsa 491 Vernon Ct., Piscataway <u>Tel</u>: (001) 732-878 9719, (001) 732-878 3840 <u>Email</u>: igvs_nj@yahoo.com • **New York:** Pūru dāsa <u>Email</u>: unclepuru108@yahoo.com • **Oregon** - **Eugene:** Puṣpadanta dāsa <u>Tel</u>: (001) 541-461-3169 <u>Email</u>: puspadanta@hotmail.com **Washington, DC:** Preaching Center, 6925 Willow Ave. NW, 20012 <u>Tel</u>: (001) 301-864-3354

AUSTRALIA: • **Murwillumbah:** <u>Email</u>: info@giriraja.org.au <u>Website</u>: www.giriraja.org.au

BOLIVA: • **Cochamba:** Raṅga Purī dāsa, PO Box 2070 <u>Tel</u>: (00591) 4-450 2132, (00591) 4-450 3467 <u>Email</u>: bbt@supernet.com.bo, epicentrohk@yahoo.com

CANADA: • **Ashcroft:** Swami Mills Preaching Center, PO. Box 323, Ashcroft, B.C. V0K1A0 <u>Tel</u>: (001) 250-457 7432 <u>Email</u>: subhadrasakha_dasa@yahoo.com

CHINA: • **Hong Kong:** Nandana dāsa, 15B Hillview court, 30 Hillwood Road, TST, Kowloon <u>Tel</u>: (0086) 852- 3422 1195, (0086) 852-9740 9846 <u>Email</u>: <u>uttamkrishna@netvigator.com</u>

COSTA RICA: • **San Jose:** Śrī Sarasvatī Prabhupāda Gauḍīya Maṭha, 1352 1ª Avenida, Cuesta de Nuṣez San Jose <u>Tel</u>: (00506) 256 8650 <u>Email</u>: horibol@sol.racsa.co.cr

FIJI ISLANDS: • **Lautoka:** Fiji Gauḍīya Maṭha, 63 Vitoga Parade <u>Tel</u>: (00679) 661 633 <u>Email</u>: jagannath@punjas.com.fj

FRANCE: • **Toulouse:** Centre de Bhakti-Yoga de Toulouse, 11, Rue Peyrolieres, 31000 <u>Tel</u>: (0033) 0561-22 17 24, (0033) 0561-68 11 69 <u>Email</u>: <u>bvsrauti@yahoo.fr</u> <u>Website</u>: bvnmenfrancais@yahoogroups.fr

GERMANY: • **Berlin:** Śrī Gaura-Nitāī Gauḍīya Maṭha <u>Tel</u>: (0049) 030-62 00 87 47 <u>Email</u>: bhaktiberlin@yahoo.de • **Stuttgart:** Vedischer Kulturverein e.v., Daimlerstrasse 61a, 70372 Stuttgart - Bad Cannstatt <u>Tel</u>: (0049) 0711-411 71 93

HOLLAND: • **Rotterdam:** Śrī Śrī Rādhā-Govinda Gauḍīya Maṭha, 1e Pijnackerstraat 98, 3035GV <u>Tel</u>: (0031) 010-265 04 05 <u>Email</u>: sanga_holland@yahoo.com

INDIA: • **Bangalore:** Śrī Ranganath Gauḍīya Maṭha, Hesseraghatta, Near Nrtyagram Kuteeram, Survey #26 <u>Mobile</u>: (0091) 080-9341 9614 91 <u>Email</u>: bangalore@purebhakti.com • **Mathurā:** Śrī Keśavajī Gauḍīya Maṭha, opp. Dist. Hospital, Jawahar Hata, U.P. 281001 <u>Tel</u>: (0091) 0565-250 2334 <u>Email</u>: mathuramath@purebhakti.com • **Govardhana:** Giridhārī Gauḍīya Maṭha, Mathurā District, Radha-kund Road, U.P. <u>Tel</u>: (0091) 0565-281 5668 • **Navadwipa:** Śrī Devānanda Gauḍīya Maṭha, Tegharipada, PO Navadwipa, D/O Nadiya, West -Bengal (0091) 0343-240 068 • **New Delhi:** Śrī Ramaṇa-vihārī Gauḍīya Maṭha, OCF pocket, Block B-3, near musical fountain park, Janakpuri <u>Tel</u>: (0091) 011-2553 3568 / (0091) 011-3230 2159 <u>Email</u>: ramchandradas2001@yahoo.com • **Vṛndāvana:** Śrī Rūpa-Sanātana Gauḍīya Maṭha, Dana Gali <u>Tel</u>: (0091) 0565-244 3270

INDONESIA: • **Bali:** Śrī Ananta Gauḍīya Maṭha, Br. Juntal, Desa Kaba-Kaba, Kediri, Tabanan <u>Tel</u>: (0062) 0361-83 09 86 <u>Email</u>: regalb@indosat.net.id

ITALY: • **Curino:** Associazione Vaiṣṇava Gauḍīya Vedānta, Līlā-Puruṣottama dāsa, Cantone Salero n.5, 13865 (BI) <u>Tel/Fax</u>: (0039) 015-928173 <u>Email</u>: gaudyait@tin.it <u>Website</u>: www.gaudiya.it

MALAYSIA: • **Selangor:** Preaching Center, 48 Jalan Gasing, 46000 Petaling Jaya <u>Tel</u>: (0060) 3-957 62 67, (0060) 12-349 85 52, (0060) 12-321 37 87 <u>Email</u>: acyutha108@myjaring.net • **Penang:** Parameśvarī dāsa, 130-C Jalan Utama (W.R.), George Town, 10350 <u>Tel</u>: (0060) 4-899 19 59, (0060) 12-401 99 39, (0060) 12-429 59 39 <u>Email</u>: kmala12@hotmail.com

NEW ZEALAND: • **Auckland:** Sri Krishna Chaitanya Ashram, 35 Whitford Park Road, Whitford Village <u>Tel</u>: (0064) 9-273 90 60 <u>Email</u>: nz@purebhakti.com

NIGERIA: • **Lagos:** Bhṛgu dāsa, 3 Johnson Close Kiri-Kiri, Apapa, Lagos <u>Tel</u>: (00234) 1-791 77 77 <u>Mobile</u>: (00234) 8033 943 642 <u>Email</u>: rkt1082000@yahoo.co.uk

PHILIPPINES: • **Manila:** (0063) 2983 3605 <u>Mobile</u>: (0063) 91 7834 5885 <u>Email</u> jaipur_art@lycos.com

SPAIN: • **Granada:** Vṛndāvaneśvarī dāsī <u>Email</u>: vrindavanesvari@gmail.com • **Madrid:** Kṛṣṇa-prema dāsa <u>Tel</u>: (0034) 91 468 60 59 <u>Email</u>: krsnaprema108@hotmail.com

SWITZERLAND: • Kṛṣṇacandra dasa <u>Tel</u>: (0041) 041-879 00 09 <u>Email</u>: radhe@patram.net <u>Website</u>: www.sanatan-dharma.ch

UNITED KINGDOM: • **England - Birmingham:** Śrī Gour-Govinda Gauḍīya Maṭha, 174-A Alcester Road, Moseley Village B13 8HJ <u>Tel</u>: (0044) 121-449 2676 <u>Email</u>: gourgovinda@hotmail.com - **London:** Gaṅgā-mātā Gauḍīya Maṭha, Kamala dāsī <u>Email</u>: gangamatajis@yahoo.com.uk • **Wales - Oakford:** Svānanda-Sukada-kuñja Temple, Sa. 470 Rd Llanarth, Ceredigion <u>Tel</u>: (0044) 15-4558 0441

For more information on other books by Śrīla Bhaktivedanta Narayana Maharaja, visit www.bhaktistore.com.

International Book Distributors

For Wholesale Inquiries, please visit www.bhaktiprojects.org or contact your local warehouse:

Australia:
Attn: Līlā-śuka dāsa
Tel: (0061) 266-797 025
Email: lilasuka@bigpond.com

Canada:
Stanley A. Gill,
#25 - 15030 58th Ave.
Surrey, B.C. CANADA V3S 9G3
Attn: Praśasya dāsa
Tel: (001) 866-575 9438
Email: stannshel@shaw.ca

Europe-UK (England)
Śrī Gour Govinda Gaudīya Math:
Attn: Jīva-pāvana dāsa,
Tel: (0044) 1536 4817 69
Email: jivapavana@aol.com

Malaysia:
Attn: Vijaya Kṛṣṇa dāsa
Tel: (0060) 012-385 42 02
       (0060) 012-321 37 87
       (0060) 012-397 37 23
Email: vjkrsna@yahoo.com

USA
Bhaktiprojects:
4589 Pacheco Blvd.
Martinez, CA 94553
Attn: Viśvambhara dāsa
Tel: 800-681 3040 ext. 108 (within U.S. only)
Email: vdasa@bhaktiprojects.org

For information on becoming a distributor in your area, please contact Viśvambhara dāsa:
Email: vdasa@bhaktiprojects.org Tel: 800-681 3040 ext. 108 (within U.S. only)